The Hunted

Has Become

The Hunter

John A. Alexander

To learn more about John's work, upcoming releases, and exclusive updates, please visit:
www.bestsellersbyjohnaalexander.com

For direct contact:
author@bestsellersbyjohnaalexander.com

Published by

Ultra Publishers
www.ultrapublishers.com

Printed in the United States of America

Dedication

After extensive research and hard work devoted to making this book the best it can be, I want to acknowledge that inspiration came easily—because so much information was available. However, the most important inspiration behind every book I write is my family.

They support me fully and trust the message I share through my work. For that reason, I dedicate this book to them—my loving wife and my three wonderful sons.

And above all, to You, my God: You are my everything. My life is lived for You alone. Thank You.

Acknowledgment

We live in a world where we face both good and evil more clearly and intensely than ever before. We see this in the United States during the Trump administration, but it is happening all over the world—in politics, governments, churches, companies, and society as a whole.

The reason I write these books is to help people see that common sense must return to our societies. We cannot continue to endorse individuals, politicians, or institutions when we clearly see evil acts taking place—attacks on truth and attacks on what is right. The warning is simple: if you participate in wrongdoing, you are contributing to the destruction of your nation and the future of the next generation—your children. But if you do your own research, seek truth, and stand for what is right, you become part of building a nation that is blessed and prosperous. In doing so, you help create a better future—one from which your children and loved ones will benefit most. That may become your greatest legacy.

I have three wonderful sons, and I am deeply concerned for them. They need God, solid education, and the ability to see reality clearly—not to be deceived by social media or networks that have shifted far from truth. They must learn to discern lies from truth and resist the evil narratives that are so widely spread today.

I wrote this book as an outsider—I am not American and do not live in the United States—after witnessing years of what I believe to be complete nonsense. Administrations were attacked for securing the border, yet little was said when borders were left open and millions were allowed to enter unchecked. Many of those decisions led to crime, and countless families suffered the loss of children to murder, rape, and other violent acts committed against innocent Americans.

I understand what it means to be attacked for doing what is right and for standing up for truth. For that reason, I was amazed by how President Donald J. Trump stood firm against relentless attacks meant to bring him down. One of the greatest miracles for anyone in such a position is to remain standing—to refuse to compromise standards under pressure. That is why I write these books: so that readers might move from being victims of misinformation to discovering truth, because truth brings freedom.

My hope is that we learn a powerful lesson—that those we attempt to destroy today may one day stand in positions of authority, not seeking revenge, but delivering justice to those who once abused their power.

I hope you enjoy this book.

About the Author

John has traveled extensively around the world, teaching and speaking to companies and religious organizations on topics that remain deeply relevant today. His lectures span a wide range of subjects—from business and politics to personal development, sales, leadership, and marriage—all with a consistent purpose: to challenge his audience to think critically, grow confidently, and strive to become better individuals in every area of life.

With more than forty years of experience influencing and inspiring people face-to-face, John is now embracing a lifelong passion—writing. Through his books, he seeks to share the lessons, insights, and wisdom he has gained over decades of teaching, leadership, and global experience.

He plans to publish four to five books each year, ensuring this is only the beginning of what readers can expect from him. John's knowledge is profound, thought-provoking, and always grounded in truth.

Table of Contents

1 John 3:18 (New King James Version)

18 My little children, let us not love in word or in tongue, but in deed and in truth.

TRUE LEADERSHIP IS NOT ABOUT SHOWING LOVE IN WORDS BUT IN DEEDS. IF YOU ARE GOING TO LEAD A PEOPLE OR A NATION, YOU MUST LOVE THE PEOPLE OF THAT NATION. THE WAY I SEE IT IS:

- God first
- God's people second
- Yourself last

God and people over party; God and people over self.

CHAPTER ONE – THE HUNTED HAS BECOME THE HUNTER

There comes a time when the tables turn—when those who were falsely accused, mocked, and attacked finally have the opportunity to stand up and expose the truth. For years, Donald J. Trump was hunted by the political establishment, the media, and those who feared the power of his influence. He was targeted not because he did wrong, but because he dared to challenge the system that had controlled Washington for decades.

They called him every name in the book. They investigated him, impeached him, and tried to destroy his reputation. Yet, through all the noise and accusations, Trump never gave up. He fought back—not out of revenge, but out of conviction that what was done to him was wrong, and what was done to the American people was even worse. He knew the fight was not just personal; it was for the soul of the nation.

Now the story has shifted. The hunted has become the hunter. The one who was chased is now the one seeking truth and justice. Trump stands in a position few men ever reach—one who knows the full power of the system that tried to break him and now has the courage to expose it for what it really is.

This is not about vengeance. This is about righting a wrong. When powerful people in government, media, or law enforcement use their authority to destroy someone for political gain, they must be held accountable. If they broke the law, they should face the same justice they tried to deny others. What Trump represents now is not a man looking to settle scores, but a man determined to make sure the American people finally see what has been hidden behind closed doors for far too long.

Every false accusation, every smear, every lie told against him has only strengthened his resolve. Trump's rise from being the hunted to the hunter is symbolic of millions of Americans who felt voiceless, powerless, and betrayed. They see in him a reflection of their own fight—people who have been silenced, labeled, and ignored by those in power. Now, through his boldness, they too are standing up, saying, "Enough is enough."

This chapter of history is about accountability. It is about showing that no one—no politician, no journalist, no bureaucrat—is above the law. It is about restoring faith in truth and justice. And it reminds us that even when it seems that evil has the upper hand, time always reveals the truth.

Donald Trump's journey from being the hunted to becoming the hunter is not just his story—it's America's story. It's about resilience, perseverance, and the courage to face the very forces that tried to destroy you. When truth becomes your weapon, you no longer need revenge. Justice itself becomes your victory.

CHAPTER TWO – THE ART OF LOYALTY

Loyalty has always been one of Donald J. Trump's most defining qualities—both in what he demands and what he gives. From the towers of Manhattan to the halls of Washington, Trump has made it clear that loyalty is not a mere virtue; it is a necessity. To him, loyalty is the test of character. It is the currency of trust. It is what separates those who build something lasting from those who are only there for the spotlight.

He built his empire surrounded by people who had proven themselves over time. Some worked for him for decades; others became trusted allies through moments of trial. Trump's philosophy was simple: if you stand by me, I will stand by you. That was the code. In his mind, loyalty was not about blind obedience, but about faith—faith in the mission, faith in the team, and faith in the man leading it.

Yet, as Trump transitioned from the world of business into the world of politics, he discovered that loyalty in Washington was far different from loyalty in New York. In business, a handshake could seal a deal. In politics, a handshake could be the beginning of betrayal. The same people who smiled in the Oval Office could turn around and leak private conversations to the press before the day was over.

THE SHOCK OF POLITICAL BETRAYAL

Trump's first years in office taught him that political loyalty often had an expiration date. Many who had pledged allegiance to his vision—"Make America Great Again"—soon found comfort in the old ways of Washington once pressure mounted. When the media storms came and the investigations began, some folded, some fled, and a few turned against him to protect themselves.

It was a brutal lesson in human nature and power. Trump saw firsthand how fear can destroy loyalty. He watched people he had trusted bow to political pressure, afraid of being labeled or targeted. He understood that loyalty, when not rooted in conviction, collapses under the weight of convenience.

Still, even through the betrayals, Trump's belief in loyalty never wavered. He knew that without loyalty, there could be no trust. Without trust, there could be no leadership. His loyalty to his supporters became his strongest weapon. When institutions turned against him, the people stood by him—millions of Americans who had never met him personally but who believed he was fighting for them.

THE LOYALTY OF THE PEOPLE

This relationship between Trump and his base is one of the most fascinating political bonds in modern history. It is not built on party loyalty but on emotional and moral loyalty. His supporters see him as one of them—flawed but fearless, wealthy yet relatable, powerful yet under attack. They trust him because he never hides who he is. They defend him because they believe he defends them.

Even when the media tried to turn the public against him, his base only grew more loyal. Every attack only confirmed what they already believed—that he was fighting a corrupt system designed to silence their voice. In a world of polished politicians, Trump's raw honesty and loyalty to his promises stood out like a storm against a quiet sky.

That is why, when others betrayed him, the people did not. His loyalty to America became their rallying cry. It was never about perfection—it was about persistence. It was about the belief that loyalty to truth, to country, and to God would ultimately prevail over deceit and hypocrisy.

LOYALTY AND LEADERSHIP

For Trump, leadership without loyalty is chaos. He values strong minds and independent thinkers, but he also expects unity of purpose. Loyalty does not mean never disagreeing; it means never abandoning. He often said that disagreements were part of progress—but betrayal was unforgivable. A team can only succeed when each member is loyal to the mission, not to personal ambition.

Trump's expectation of loyalty was often misunderstood by his critics. They saw it as arrogance or control. But those who understood him closely knew it came from a place of trust and responsibility. He demanded loyalty because he was willing to give it—and because he had seen how disloyalty can destroy movements, families, and nations.

Loyalty, to Trump, is not weakness—it is strength. It is the foundation that allows risk, innovation, and courage to flourish. A leader surrounded by loyal people can withstand storms that would destroy others. And Trump, more than anyone, has weathered more storms than most men could endure.

THE TEST OF TRUE LOYALTY

In the end, loyalty is tested not in times of peace, but in times of war—not when things are easy, but when everything is on the line. Trump's entire journey in politics has been one long test of loyalty—from those closest to him, from those who served under him, and from those who voted for him.

And while many failed that test, others rose to meet it. Those who stood with him when it cost them everything became part of a legacy that transcends politics. They became part of something historical—a movement that values faith, honesty, and country above power.

The art of loyalty is not about perfection. It is about perseverance. It is about knowing who you are and who you stand with when the world turns against you. Trump continues to show that loyalty is the true measure of a man—and that, in the end, it is the loyal, not the loud, who change history.

CHAPTER THREE – THE PRICE OF POWER

Power is a gift few men ever truly understand until they hold it in their hands. For Donald J. Trump, power was never something to be feared—it was something to be used. But as he would discover, the higher a man rises, the more it costs to stay there. Every decision, every word, every alliance carries a price. And for Trump, the price of power was steep—not just in politics, but in life itself.

Trump's relationship with power began long before the presidency. In the business world, power was measured by vision, results, and boldness. He earned it through determination, not privilege. He took risks others avoided and won deals others said were impossible. Yet even then, he learned that power attracts both loyalty and envy. The same people who applauded his success often waited for a chance to see him fail.

When he entered the political arena, that truth multiplied a hundredfold. Power in Washington is a different kind of beast. It is built not on creation but on control—not on results, but on influence. The more Trump sought to change the system, the more the system pushed back. His rise to the presidency was not welcomed by the establishment; it was seen as a direct threat to their survival.

THE ISOLATION OF LEADERSHIP

One of the hardest lessons of power is loneliness. The higher you climb, the fewer people you can truly trust. Trump discovered that quickly. As president, he carried the hopes of millions who wanted to see America restored to strength, yet behind the scenes he faced resistance at every turn—even from within his own administration.

He learned that being right did not guarantee support. He learned that truth, when it threatens comfort, is often ignored. Many who claimed to stand with him when the cameras were on were nowhere to be found when the real battles began. That is the price of power—standing alone in the storm, knowing that leadership often means losing the comfort of friendship and approval.

But Trump's strength was his ability to endure that isolation. He never needed the approval of the elite. He found his connection not in the halls of power but in the crowds of everyday Americans who saw in him something rare—a man willing to fight for them no matter the cost.

THE COST TO FAMILY AND REPUTATION

Every great leader pays a personal price for public power. Trump's family was no exception. His children were mocked, his wife unfairly attacked, his businesses investigated—all as part of the price he paid for challenging the establishment. In the eyes of his enemies, nothing was off-limits. His success in politics made him a target not only as a leader but as a father and husband.

Yet through it all, his family remained his anchor. They endured the criticism and stood by him through every false accusation. They understood that greatness demands sacrifice. Trump himself often said that the cost of doing what is right can be painful, but that the reward—integrity—is worth far more than comfort or popularity.

THE MORAL BURDEN OF POWER

With power comes the constant test of character. It exposes a man's true motives. For Trump, the test was not whether he could gain power, but whether he could use it for something greater than himself. His presidency revealed how deeply he believed that power should serve the people, not the politicians. So true.

He refused to accept that America's strength had to come at the expense of its people. He challenged global deals that weakened the nation, demanded accountability from foreign allies, and stood up to critics who said his style was too aggressive. He

believed that moral leadership sometimes required confrontation—
that peace without truth is not peace at all.

But Trump also knew that moral conviction would bring
opposition. Those who thrive on corruption will always hate those
who expose it. That hatred was part of his price—and he paid it
willingly.

POWER AND PURPOSE

At its core, Trump's story is about purpose. Power without
purpose is corruption; power with purpose becomes destiny. His
purpose was to restore faith in the American spirit—to remind
people that greatness is not inherited, it is earned. And to do that,
he had to walk through fire.

Every attack, every investigation, every false story written
about him became another test of how much he was willing to
endure for what he believed. He could have chosen comfort. He
could have walked away, and was perhaps tempted to do so many
times. But Trump understood something most people never do—
that when you are chosen for a mission larger than yourself,
quitting is not an option. It is not in his vocabulary.

THE LEGACY OF THE PRICE

History often remembers power by what it achieves, but it
should also remember what it costs. Trump's legacy will not just

be written in policies or victories; it will be written in perseverance. His endurance under relentless opposition revealed the true cost of leadership in an age of corruption and division.

The price of power is loneliness, sacrifice, and constant scrutiny. But it is also the opportunity to do what others are afraid to do—to tell the truth when lies are easier, to stand when others kneel, and to keep fighting when the world says it's over.

Trump has paid that price again and again, yet he continues forward. For him, power is not about personal gain. It is about purpose, faith, and the belief that one man can still make a difference. And in paying that price, he has reminded America— and the world—that real power does not corrupt the honest; it reveals the brave.

CHAPTER FOUR – DEALMAKER-IN-CHIEF

From the earliest days of his career, Donald J. Trump saw the world through the lens of a negotiator. Every opportunity was a deal waiting to be made, every challenge a chance to prove that the impossible could be achieved with the right mix of courage, leverage, and confidence. Long before he became president, Trump had already mastered the art of persuasion—not just in business, but in life itself.

He wrote about it, lived it, and embodied it. His 1987 book *The Art of the Deal* wasn't simply a memoir—it was a blueprint for how he saw the world. Deals weren't just transactions; they were relationships built on timing, power, and instinct. He believed that negotiation was not about pleasing everyone, but about creating win-win outcomes through strength. And that mindset, when brought into the Oval Office, changed everything.

NEGOTIATION AS STRATEGY

When Trump entered the White House, he didn't abandon his business instincts—he refined them. He viewed every political challenge, trade deal, or diplomatic discussion as a negotiation. Whether sitting across from corporate executives, political opponents, or world leaders, Trump always sought leverage first. He understood something many politicians never did: negotiation is not about talk; it's about position.

His philosophy was simple—never go into a deal without knowing your worth. Trump applied that rule to America itself. He looked at international agreements, trade policies, and defense alliances and asked the question few dared to ask: Is America winning? If the answer was no, he renegotiated. Whether it was NAFTA, NATO, or trade with China, he believed that a strong America was one that stood its ground and demanded fairness.

His critics accused him of being too blunt, too bold, too confrontational. But those who understood business recognized the strategy. Trump knew that in any deal, strength earns respect, and weakness invites manipulation. He did not seek to make everyone like him; he sought to make everyone respect the United States again.

THE POWER OF PERCEPTION

In negotiation, perception is reality. Trump understood that better than anyone. He built his brand—and later his presidency— on the power of image, confidence, and control. Whether through television, social media, or public events, he knew that how you present yourself determines how others treat you.

That's why he never allowed his opponents to define him. When attacked, he countered. When mocked, he doubled down. To Trump, negotiation wasn't just at the table; it was in the public arena. The media was another battlefield, and he negotiated perception with the same ferocity he brought to financial deals.

His famous "America First" slogan was itself a negotiation stance. It told the world that America would no longer settle for less, that the days of one-sided deals were over. He used words the way a builder uses steel—to construct something durable. Even his tweets, often criticized, were part of his strategy: shaping narrative, controlling timing, and keeping opponents off balance.

THE BUSINESS OF POLITICS

To many in Washington, Trump's approach was shocking. They were used to compromise for the sake of optics. Trump believed in compromise only when it strengthened the nation. He did not see politics as theater—he saw it as business, with results that directly affected millions of lives.

He demanded accountability the same way he did in his companies. He expected results, deadlines, and measurable progress. Those who worked under him quickly learned that excuses were not acceptable. If a plan didn't work, fix it. If a policy failed, adjust it. But don't quit.

That direct style disrupted a culture of complacency that had dominated politics for decades. Trump's focus on performance and loyalty created tension, but it also delivered results. Unemployment dropped, the economy surged, and America's global standing shifted from passive to powerful.

THE ART OF LEVERAGE

Every deal Trump made, from Manhattan real estate to the Middle East peace accords, followed the same principle—find leverage and use it. In his view, leverage wasn't manipulation; it was clarity. Knowing what you have, what you need, and what the other side wants gives you control.

In foreign policy, leverage meant understanding that America's strength was not something to apologize for—it was something to use. He reminded allies that partnership must be mutual, not one-sided. He stood firm with adversaries, not to provoke, but to show that America's word still carried weight.

Trump's negotiations with nations like China, North Korea, and Iran demonstrated that even in a world of complex diplomacy, the core rules of the deal never change: know your goals, know your limits, and never let fear dictate your terms.

THE HUMAN SIDE OF THE DEAL

Yet behind the sharp tone and relentless drive was a man who understood people. Trump's greatest deals were built not only on numbers, but on instinct. He read people—their motives, fears, and ambitions—and used that understanding to connect and lead.

Even his harshest critics admitted that in person, Trump could be surprisingly charming, gracious, and persuasive. He believed that business and politics both came down to relationships—and relationships were about trust, respect, and the courage to say "no" when it mattered most.

LEGACY OF THE DEALMAKER

When history remembers Donald Trump, it will not just recall his time in office or his political battles. It will remember the man who brought a dealmaker's heart into a world ruled by talkers—a man who reminded America that leadership is not about appeasement, but about conviction.

Trump showed that negotiation, when rooted in strength and purpose, can rebuild economies, restore dignity, and reshape history. He reminded a weary nation that the greatest deal of all is not written on paper—it's written in courage.

He proved that sometimes, the best deal isn't the one that pleases everyone. It's the one that protects what matters most. And for Trump, that deal was—and will always be—America.

CHAPTER FIVE – THE MEDIA BATTLEFIELD

Long before he entered politics, Donald J. Trump understood one unshakable truth—the media is the most powerful weapon in America. It can destroy reputations, move markets, and shape nations. He had studied it, mastered it, and used it to build his empire long before he ever ran for president. But when he stepped into the political arena, he discovered that the same media that once elevated him was now determined to take him down.

Trump's relationship with the media is one of the most fascinating and complex in modern history. He was both its creation and its critic, its obsession and its adversary. He understood the rules of exposure better than anyone—that attention is power, and power attracts attention. The media wanted stories that sold, and Trump knew how to give them that. But what he didn't anticipate was how deeply the media establishment would unite against him once he threatened their control over public perception.

THE MEDIA'S OBSESSION

From the moment Trump announced his candidacy in 2015, the cameras never stopped rolling. Networks that once dismissed him as a joke soon realized he was ratings gold. Every rally, every statement, every controversy drew millions of viewers. The media covered him relentlessly, and in doing so, helped make him the most talked-about man on the planet.

But what began as fascination quickly turned into hostility. As Trump gained political traction, many in the press realized that his rise represented a direct threat to the old order. He wasn't just challenging the political elite—he was exposing the media's bias, their selective reporting, and their control over information.

He called them out in front of the world, labeling them "fake news." The term became a cultural lightning bolt, a phrase that split the nation. To his critics, it was an attack on the free press. To his supporters, it was the truth finally spoken aloud. For the first time, millions of Americans began questioning what they read and watched, realizing that news was often narrative—not fact.

WEAPONIZING THE SPOTLIGHT

Trump did not run from the media war; he ran straight into it. He understood that in a world driven by headlines, silence is defeat. So he did what no politician had ever done—he turned the media's attacks into free publicity. He was now the HUNTER, bolder and unwilling to bow down to the media or the corruption around him.

Every insult, every accusation, every false headline became fuel. When reporters criticized him, he responded directly. When networks cut his speeches, he went to Twitter. He refused to let them dictate his story. In doing so, he reshaped the battlefield.

For Trump, the media was not the enemy—it was the arena. He realized that if he could not control what they said about him, he could at least control the conversation. By staying unpredictable, bold, and relentless, he kept the media chasing his every move. He understood that in politics, whoever dominates attention dominates the game.

THE POWER OF AUTHENTICITY

One of Trump's greatest media strengths was his authenticity. He didn't speak like a politician; he spoke like a man having a conversation. His tone was raw, direct, and often controversial, but it was real. In an age of scripted speeches and rehearsed soundbites, that authenticity made him impossible to ignore.

The press tried to use his unfiltered style against him, yet that same quality made him relatable to millions. Voters saw him not as a polished insider, but as one of them—flawed, passionate, and unafraid to speak his mind. His willingness to break media protocol became his greatest weapon, turning what others saw as weakness into strength.

He proved that media power no longer belonged to those who owned the networks, but to those who owned their message.

SOCIAL MEDIA: THE NEW FRONTLINE

No leader in history has used social media as effectively as Donald Trump. His Twitter feed became a direct line to the American people, bypassing traditional media filters. While the press analyzed and twisted his words, he spoke directly to millions in real time.

Every tweet became a headline, every message a statement of dominance. He forced the media to react to him instead of the other way around. By doing so, he reversed decades of control, making journalists follow his lead rather than shape his image.

Trump's mastery of digital communication transformed politics forever. It showed future leaders that the power of narrative had shifted—from television studios to smartphones, from networks to individuals.

THE WAR OF PERCEPTION

Trump's media battles were never just about coverage; they were about control of truth itself. He recognized that the media had long shaped reality by selecting what to show and what to hide. He challenged that power head-on, forcing Americans to see how stories were manipulated, edited, and spun for agenda rather than honesty.

His presidency became a war of perception—a constant clash between image and reality, between truth and narrative. And although the media claimed to hold him accountable, history may one day show that it was Trump who held them accountable.

REDEFINING THE PRESS

By the end of his presidency, Trump had changed journalism in ways few could have imagined. He exposed bias, revealed hypocrisy, and broke the illusion of neutrality. Even his harshest critics had to admit that he made the media answer for its own corruption.

He reminded the world that freedom of the press is sacred— but so is the freedom to question it.

Trump's war with the media was not just personal; it was philosophical. It was a battle for truth in an age of noise. It was about restoring the power of discernment to the people—teaching them to see beyond headlines and to think for themselves.

And in that fight, Trump emerged not as the victim, but as the victor—because he proved that no amount of negative press can silence a man who refuses to be defined by it.

LEGACY OF THE BATTLEFIELD

Donald J. Trump's media war will be studied for generations. It redefined politics, communication, and power itself. He taught the world that control of the narrative is the ultimate weapon—and that authenticity, boldness, and courage can defeat even the most coordinated opposition.

In a world where perception often outweighs truth, Trump stood as a reminder that real strength lies not in popularity, but in perseverance. The media may have tried to destroy him, but in the end, he became their greatest story—the man they could never ignore, never silence, and never defeat.

CHAPTER SIX – FAITH, MORALITY, AND POLITICS

Faith and morality have always stood at the crossroads of American leadership. They shape how a nation governs, how its people unite, and how its leaders are remembered. For Donald J. Trump, faith was not something worn like a badge—it was a force tested through fire. His journey through business, politics, and global scrutiny became a living example of how moral conviction can both elevate and challenge a man in power.

Trump's rise to leadership did not come through traditional pathways of religion or politics. He was not a preacher, nor did he pretend to be one. Yet from the beginning of his presidency, people of faith recognized something in him—a man unafraid to speak about God, justice, and the spiritual decay that had taken hold of the nation. To many, he was not the perfect man for the job, but the chosen man for the moment. I believe that God was molding him for such a time as this. Even though many Christians at first rejected him, one thing they never understood was that his position was not that of a pastor or spiritual leader but rather that he would lead in a way that made a greater impact than many spiritual leaders have done. God would use him to protect the rights of Christians. As mentioned in my other books, this is a Season of Grace, a time when God chooses an ordinary man to fight for America.

FAITH IN THE PUBLIC ARENA

In an era when most politicians avoided public displays of faith for fear of controversy, Trump did the opposite. He openly spoke about the importance of prayer, the defense of religious freedom, and the need to protect America's Christian heritage. He reminded the nation that faith was not something to hide—it was something to defend.

He surrounded himself with spiritual advisors, pastors, and leaders from various denominations who prayed with him, encouraged him, and guided him through some of the most difficult years of his life. For many of them, Trump's openness to faith was not about image—it was about humility. He was willing to listen to God's people, even when he didn't claim to be one of them.

Trump understood that faith and politics were inseparable in America's foundation. The moral compass of a nation is not set in the halls of government but in the hearts of its people. And he saw clearly that when faith is silenced, corruption grows, and truth becomes negotiable.

THE MORAL CONFLICT OF LEADERSHIP

Every leader faces moral tests, but for Trump, those tests were magnified under the relentless glare of global attention. His life was dissected, his words twisted, his past weaponized. Yet in the midst of that storm, Trump never claimed perfection. He often said, "I'm not a saint," but he stood firm for the principles that shaped his vision of America—faith, family, hard work, and national pride.

He represented millions who felt unseen—Christians, conservatives, and ordinary Americans who believed morality had become a target in the modern age. Trump gave them a voice. He defended the unborn, supported Israel, and spoke boldly against political correctness that sought to erase moral boundaries.

Still, his journey forced the nation to confront an uncomfortable truth: can a flawed man still be used for a righteous purpose? History answers yes. From biblical kings to modern leaders, God often works through imperfect vessels to achieve divine outcomes. Trump's leadership was no exception. His flaws made him relatable; his convictions made him powerful.

FAITH UNDER FIRE

During his presidency, Trump faced attacks not just on his policies but on his character. Many in the media mocked his expressions of faith, labeling them insincere. Critics pointed to his imperfections while ignoring the moral decay of the very systems he fought against. Yet through it all, he never turned away from the spiritual side of his mission.

He continued to invite prayer into the White House, to defend pastors' rights to speak freely, and to ensure that religious organizations could operate without government interference. He believed that when the government oversteps into faith, tyranny begins.

His policies reflected that conviction. From protecting Christian values to standing against the persecution of believers worldwide, Trump made it clear that faith was not just personal—it was national.

THE BATTLE FOR MORALITY IN MODERN AMERICA

Trump's presidency became a mirror reflecting the moral struggle of a nation. On one side stood those who wanted to remove God from public life, redefine truth, and replace conviction with convenience. On the other stood those who still believed in right and wrong, in good and evil, in accountability before God and man.

Trump's boldness reignited that debate. He exposed hypocrisy in both political and religious institutions, reminding Americans that morality cannot exist without courage. He showed that leadership is not about perfection but about direction—about moving a people toward truth even when the cost is high.

FAITH AS THE FOUNDATION OF FREEDOM

For Trump, faith was more than a personal belief; it was the foundation of freedom itself. He understood that without faith, freedom dies—because when people no longer believe in something higher than government, they become slaves to it. His speeches often echoed the idea that America's greatness was not born from wealth or power but from a deep trust in God.

He once said, "We don't worship government, we worship God." That simple phrase became a declaration of independence for millions of Americans who felt their faith was under siege. It reminded them that liberty is not given by politicians but granted by the Creator.

LEGACY OF CONVICTION

Trump's legacy in faith and morality will not be measured by the approval of theologians or pundits but by the millions whose courage was reignited because of him. He made believers bolder, pastors stronger, and citizens more aware of the spiritual war within their nation.

He reminded the world that God does not call the perfect—He calls the willing. And in answering that call, Trump carried the torch of faith into one of the darkest moral battles of our time.

His journey proves that morality and power need not be enemies, and that even in politics, faith still moves mountains.

CHAPTER SEVEN – THE LOYAL BASE

Few political movements in modern history have inspired loyalty like the one surrounding Donald J. Trump. It is not a campaign, nor a fleeting political wave—it is a living force, a shared belief system that transcends party lines and traditional politics. Trump's supporters are not bound by ideology alone; they are united by something far more personal—trust.

This trust was not built overnight. It was earned through years of watching a man take the blows that others would have avoided and still refuse to back down. For millions of Americans, Trump became a voice for those who felt voiceless, a defender of values they believed were slipping away. He said what others would not, and he fought battles others were afraid to fight. In him, they saw not just a leader, but a reflection of themselves—flawed, resilient, and unwilling to surrender.

A MOVEMENT, NOT A MOMENT

What began as a campaign in 2015 quickly evolved into something deeper—a national awakening. People from every background—business owners, farmers, veterans, churchgoers, and everyday citizens—found themselves drawn to a message that spoke directly to their hearts: America First. I wish other countries, including mine, would embrace such principles: Canada First, UK First, England First, Argentina First, El Salvador First, and so on. Why would governments do anything different, you may ask? Because they are not for their countries but for themselves or their party.

To them, Trump was not just a politician; he was a fighter. They admired his strength, his refusal to apologize for his success, and his determination to restore dignity to a country that many felt had been ignored by its own leaders. They saw his confidence not as arrogance but as courage—the kind of courage needed to stand against a powerful and corrupt establishment.

The rallies became more than political gatherings—they were family reunions of shared belief and hope. People traveled for hours, even days, to hear him speak. They waved flags, wore red hats, and proudly declared their loyalty, not just to a man, but to the principles he represented: faith, freedom, and fairness.

WHY THEY STAND BY HIM

Loyalty to Trump is not blind devotion. It is rooted in understanding. His supporters know his flaws. They've seen his missteps, his bluntness, his controversies—and they remain. Because loyalty, real loyalty, is not about perfection; it is about truth.

They trust Trump because he never pretends to be something he's not. He speaks plainly, sometimes harshly, but always honestly. In a political world filled with polished lies and rehearsed empathy, Trump's raw authenticity became refreshing. His supporters believe him because he tells them what he really thinks—not what the polls tell him to say.

They saw him endure years of media attacks, endless investigations, and betrayal from within his own party. Yet through it all, he never quit. To them, that endurance proved his sincerity. They understood that no man would endure such persecution unless he truly believed in what he was fighting for.

FAITH AND IDENTITY

For many, Trump's leadership took on a spiritual dimension. He became a symbol of divine purpose—a flawed but chosen instrument in a time of moral confusion. Churches prayed for him. Pastors spoke of him from pulpits. To believers, his courage was not political but prophetic, a sign that God still raises leaders to defend truth in a fallen world.

This spiritual loyalty deepened as they saw the hatred directed toward him. The more he was attacked, the more they felt that his struggle was their struggle—that standing by him was a stand for righteousness itself. It wasn't about personality anymore; it was about purpose.

That's the reason we write these books to America—to help their cause, to stand not for a perfect party or man, but to stand as outsiders for common sense, to allow Americans to see how the world sees them. Many, of course, do not care about how we see them, but the truth of the matter is, we see it as warning those in a burning building who don't realize they are about to be destroyed. We see it as sounding an alarm, blowing the trumpet, a wake-up call.

THE PEOPLE THE ELITE FORGOT

Trump's loyal base is made up of those who had long been forgotten—factory workers, truck drivers, farmers, and small business owners who built America but were left behind by global policies and self-serving politicians. They watched their towns fade, their industries close, and their traditions mocked.

Then came a man who not only saw them but spoke for them. He reminded them that patriotism was not a sin, that working with your hands was honorable, and that faith in God was not something to be ashamed of. He called them "the forgotten men and women of America," and they never forgot that he remembered them.

That phrase—"the forgotten"—became a rallying cry. It turned frustration into faith, division into determination. Trump didn't create their loyalty; he awakened it.

A FAMILY, NOT A FANDOM

What makes Trump's movement unique is its emotional bond. Supporters see each other not as strangers but as family. They share values, fears, and hopes. When one is attacked, all feel the impact. When Trump is criticized, they take it personally, because in their eyes, attacks on him are attacks on what they believe in.

At rallies, friendships form, prayers are shared, and tears are shed. It's a movement fueled by heart, not politics. It is the America that still believes in God, country, and community—the America that refuses to be divided by race, class, or ideology.

LOYALTY TESTED AND PROVEN

Every year, every scandal, every media storm has only made this base stronger. When others would have abandoned a leader under pressure, they stood taller. Because they saw something deeper—a fight between good and evil, truth and deception, freedom and control.

Their loyalty is not just to Trump the man, but to Trump the mission—to restore integrity, pride, and moral order to a nation that had lost its way.

LEGACY OF THE LOYAL

History may call them the most loyal political movement in modern times. But they see themselves simply as Americans who love their country and the man who dared to stand up for it.

Their loyalty is not blind; it is earned. It is not built on worship, but on shared belief—that one man, through faith, courage, and perseverance, can challenge the most powerful institutions on earth and still stand.

Trump's loyal base is not going away. It is growing, evolving, and preparing. Because their loyalty was never about one election—it was about a cause that lives on.

And as Trump continues his journey, they remain behind him—not as followers, but as patriots standing shoulder to shoulder with the man who reminded them that America's greatness was never gone—it was simply waiting to be believed in again.

CHAPTER EIGHT – THE ENEMIES WITHIN

Every nation faces threats from abroad, but the most dangerous enemies are rarely the ones launching missiles or marching armies. The greatest threats are internal—hidden in the halls of power, disguised behind titles, institutions, and positions of influence. America's most destructive battles have never been fought on foreign soil; they've been fought within its own borders, against those who claim to serve the nation while secretly working against it.

Donald J. Trump understood this more than any modern leader. When he entered Washington, he expected political opposition. What he did not expect was the coordinated resistance coming from those who were supposed to be on his side—insiders, bureaucrats, advisors, and career operatives who lived in the shadows of the system. These were not political opponents; they were embedded obstacles whose loyalties were tied not to the American people but to the preservation of their own power.

THE HIDDEN GOVERNMENT

The "swamp" was not a metaphor—it was a reality. For decades, unelected individuals had gained more authority than elected representatives. Agencies had become kingdoms. Departments acted like empires. Decisions affecting millions were made in backrooms by people whose names the public would never know.

When Trump stepped into office, he disrupted this comfort. He asked questions no one had dared to ask. He demanded accountability. He exposed corruption. He cut through layers of bureaucracy that had been carefully built to protect the elite, not the people.

The response was immediate—and vicious.

Leaked documents. False narratives. Manufactured scandals. Anonymous sources. Internal sabotage.

It wasn't political disagreement. It was self-preservation from those who feared losing their influence.

THE COST OF EXPOSING TRUTH

Trump threatened something deeper than party politics: he threatened the internal ecosystem of career insiders who believed Washington belonged to them. These were individuals who thrived in secrecy, who prospered in confusion, who relied on an uninformed public.

They were not elected, yet they determined policies. They were not accountable, yet they controlled budgets. They were not visible, yet they shaped the nation.

To them, Trump was not just a president—he was a problem that had to be neutralized.

THE REAL COLLISION

The greatest battles Trump fought were not with Democrats, foreign leaders, or media networks. They were with:

Intelligence officials who weaponized their authority

Bureaucrats who stalled his directives

Advisors who pretended loyalty but leaked at night

Judges who legislated from the bench

Agencies that acted as independent governments

These were the true enemies within—the ones who viewed Trump as an intruder threatening their private kingdom.

THE SPIRITUAL NATURE OF THE FIGHT

On the surface, this battle looked political. But spiritually, it was far deeper.

Trump represented disruption. Light entering darkness. Truth entering the place where deception had been comfortable for decades.

Spiritual battles rarely come from the outside—they emerge from the places where truth threatens established lies. This was no ordinary presidency; it was a confrontation between transparency and corruption.

A SYSTEM RESISTING CHANGE

The most dangerous enemy is the one who smiles in the meeting and then works against you in silence. Trump experienced this daily. Advisors would nod in agreement, then undermine his message the moment the door closed. Policies would be blocked without explanation. Key decisions were intentionally delayed.

This wasn't incompetence—it was resistance.

And Trump, unlike past leaders, refused to play their game.

WHY THE ENEMIES FEARED HIM

They feared him because:

He owed them nothing.

He couldn't be controlled.

He wasn't afraid to expose their secrets.

He operated outside of their political culture.

He spoke directly to the people instead of through them.

The establishment thrives on middlemen. Trump eliminated them.

THE PEOPLE'S REALIZATION

As Americans watched the attacks unfold, something extraordinary happened: millions finally saw the truth.

They saw how quickly false accusations could be manufactured.

They saw how united the media and bureaucrats were against one man.

They saw how powerful hidden forces could become when threatened.

It awakened the nation.

The enemy was not Trump—the enemy was the system fighting him.

A NECESSARY BATTLE

Trump's confrontation with these inner enemies was not in vain. He exposed them. He weakened their grip. He forced them into the light. And most importantly, he awakened millions who now understand that America's future does not depend on defeating foreign nations—it depends on confronting the corruption within its own institutions.

This chapter of American history will be remembered as the moment the people discovered the truth:

The real threat to freedom was never outside the country—it was inside.

CHAPTER NINE – AMERICA FIRST, THE WORLD NEXT

When Donald J. Trump declared, "America First," the political class gasped. They treated it as a threat, a radical departure from global norms. But to the American people, those two words were not a slogan—they were a long-overdue promise. For decades, America had been used, drained, and manipulated by foreign powers who saw the nation not as a partner but as a resource to exploit. Trump's declaration was a historic reset: the era of America carrying the world on its back was over.

He was not rejecting global leadership—he was redefining it.

Under Trump, America would no longer apologize for its success or fund its own decline. Instead, it would lead from a position of strength, sovereignty, and self-respect. That shift triggered shockwaves around the world, forcing nations to rethink their strategies, alliances, and expectations. America First didn't isolate the nation—it awakened it.

THE BROKEN PROMISES OF GLOBALISM

For years, leaders promised that globalism would make America stronger. Factories closed. Jobs vanished. Towns collapsed. Trade deals were written that helped foreign economies rise while American workers fell. Politicians allowed it because they were more loyal to international institutions than to their own citizens.

Trump disrupted that illusion.

He exposed the truth: America wasn't declining because it lacked talent or capability—it was declining because its leaders chose the world over their own people.

America First became the correction to decades of misplaced priorities.

RESTORING AMERICA'S POSITION

Nothing defined Trump's approach more than his willingness to renegotiate—or walk away.

NAFTA was replaced with USMCA.

NATO was pressured to pay its fair share.

China was confronted for decades of theft and manipulation.

The Paris Climate Agreement was rejected for being economically unfair.

Billions previously sent to foreign nations were redirected back into American communities.

Trump made it clear: America would no longer be the world's piggy bank. By demanding fairness, he restored something the world had forgotten— Respect for American strength.

HOW THE WORLD RESPONDED

Contrary to media fearmongering, Trump's America First policies did not push the world away—they brought it to the negotiating table.

Leaders who once took advantage of America now had to engage with it honestly. Nations that ignored trade rules began complying. Countries that expected military support learned they had to contribute.

America First wasn't selfish—it was strategic.

It showed the world that America was done doing business at a loss. If allies wanted partnership, they needed to bring value. If adversaries wanted peace, they needed to respect boundaries. Trump rebalanced global power without firing a shot.

A NEW FORM OF RESPECT

For decades, foreign leaders studied America's weakness—the predictable diplomacy, the apologetic posture, the fear of confrontation. With Trump, that era ended.

They encountered a leader who:

- Spoke plainly
- Negotiated aggressively
- Understood leverage
- Could not be bribed with political favors

Would walk away from any deal that weakened America

They respected him—even if they didn't like him—because strength commands attention, while weakness invites manipulation.

THE FEAR OF A STRONG AMERICA

Many global players feared Trump, not because he was unpredictable, but because he was unbuyable. Global institutions thrive when America is compliant. Trump wasn't. He challenged the rules they wrote for themselves. He refused to bow to multinational corporations, global banks, and international councils that had been influencing policy for decades.

He reminded the world that America was not created to be managed by foreign entities—it was created to lead itself.

REDEFINING GLOBAL RESPONSIBILITY

Trump believed that America had a responsibility—not to police the world, but to set an example of strength, independence, and principled leadership. A strong America meant a safer world. A prosperous America meant global stability. America First did not mean America alone—it meant America in its rightful position.

And as America rose, something surprising happened:

Other nations began adopting their own versions of "country first" movements. Leaders from Europe to Latin America began putting the needs of their citizens before international pressure. Trump didn't just redefine America—he reshaped global politics.

THE GLOBAL POWER SHIFT

Under Trump, the world witnessed a rare phenomenon: a nation regaining its identity. International observers saw America standing tall again, negotiating from power, not guilt. This shift signaled to the world that leadership was no longer a performance—it was a responsibility.

Trump's influence extended beyond borders because he demonstrated what real sovereignty looks like. And in doing so, he broke the illusion that globalism was the only path forward.

AMERICA FIRST WAS NEVER ABOUT ISOLATION

It was about the simple but powerful belief that a nation must take care of its own people before it can help others. Trump proved that when a leader stands firm, the respect of the world rises.

America First reminded nations that patriotism is not extremism—it is duty.

And as the world watched America reclaim its place, it became clear:

- A strong America strengthens the world.
- A weak America endangers it.
- Trump chose strength.

CHAPTER TEN – JUSTICE, NOT REVENGE

There is a moment in every battle when the fighter must decide what he truly seeks: retaliation or righteousness. For Donald J. Trump, that moment came after years of relentless attacks—false investigations, political ambushes, media distortions, and personal assaults meant to break him. But instead of bending under pressure or seeking to settle personal scores, Trump made a choice that few expected:

He chose justice over revenge.

This decision defined the next phase of his leadership. It transformed him from a man under siege into a man on a mission—not to destroy his enemies, but to expose them. Not to punish, but to reveal. Not to strike back, but to correct a system that had been corrupted long before he ever entered politics.

Revenge is emotional.

Justice is principled.

Revenge is temporary.

Justice is transformational.

Trump understood the difference—and so did the millions who stood with him.

THE POWER OF RESTRAINT

When a man is attacked the way Trump was attacked, revenge becomes the natural response. Yet Trump knew that if he acted out of anger, he would become no different than the system that wronged him. Revenge would satisfy emotion, but it would not heal the nation. It would feed division rather than cure it. It would perpetuate the same corruption he fought against.

Trump chose a higher path: Americans over everything else.

He focused not on punishing individuals, but on fixing the environment that allowed injustice to thrive. He knew that if corruption was not exposed and dismantled, it would continue— today against him, tomorrow against the American people.

Justice required patience.

Justice required strategy.

Justice required truth.

THE DIFFERENCE BETWEEN ATTACK AND ACCOUNTABILITY

Throughout his presidency and beyond, Trump was portrayed as a man driven by ego. But those who studied his actions closely, as we did, saw something entirely different. His goal was not to damage those who opposed him, but to hold accountable those who abused their power. There is a world of difference between vengeance and accountability.

Revenge seeks to hurt someone.

Accountability seeks to prevent harm from continuing.

Trump was not interested in political payback. He was interested in justice for the American people—the people who had been lied to, manipulated, and ignored for decades by the very institutions meant to protect them.

THE SYSTEM THAT TURNED AGAINST HIM

One of the hardest truths Trump exposed was that corruption exists not just among political rivals, but within the institutions Americans trusted the most. Government agencies, intelligence departments, the justice system, and parts of law enforcement became political weapons aimed at silencing a threat, not enforcing the law.

This was not justice. This was weaponization. And Trump became the most visible victim of it.

Instead of seeking personal revenge, he made exposing the weaponization itself the mission. He made it visible. He brought it into the light. He forced Americans to see how deeply the system had been compromised.

The point was not to punish individuals—the point was to protect the Republic.

THE MORAL HIGH GROUND

There is a reason Trump's message resonates so deeply with people of faith. Revenge is a human impulse. Justice is a divine principle. Justice is rooted in truth, accountability, responsibility, and righteousness.

Trump never pretended to be perfect, but he understood one essential truth:

A nation without justice cannot survive.

He refused to use his position to destroy people for personal satisfaction. Instead, he fought for transparency, fairness, and the restoration of a justice system that serves all people, not just the elite.

This elevated him above pettiness and placed him in the realm of purpose.

WHY HIS ENEMIES FEAR "JUSTICE" MORE THAN "REVENGE"

Revenge is predictable. It is emotional. It can be manipulated.

Justice, however, is dangerous to the corrupt.

Justice is patient.

Justice is precise.

Justice brings exposure.

Justice brings consequences that last.

The system could survive Trump's anger. It could not survive Trump's commitment to truth.

That is why the opposition intensified when Trump shifted from defending himself to exposing the system. They feared what he might reveal. They feared what the people would learn. They feared that justice—real justice—would dismantle everything they had built.

JUSTICE AS A LEGACY

History will not remember Trump for the attacks against him. It will remember him for how he responded. His legacy is not rooted in retaliation—it is rooted in his determination to create a fairer, more honest, more accountable nation.

He demonstrated a truth that resonates across time:

A leader's greatness is not measured by how he fights his enemies, but by how he protects his people.

Trump's fight is not personal—it is national. Not emotional—but moral. Not short-term—but generational.

THE TRANSFORMATION FROM VICTIM TO VINDICATOR

The hunted became the hunter not by striking back in anger, but by standing firm in his purpose. Trump transformed his suffering into strategy, his pain into purpose, and his attacks into awareness for millions.

He didn't seek revenge. He sought restoration. He didn't seek to punish. He sought to correct. He didn't seek to destroy. He sought to rebuild what had been broken. That is leadership. That is moral discipline. That is justice. And justice, once awakened, cannot be stopped.

CHAPTER ELEVEN – THE GLOBAL AWAKENING

The world watched as Donald J. Trump entered the political arena and faced a level of hostility no modern leader had ever endured. But what many underestimated was the ripple effect his fight would create beyond America's borders. What began as a political storm in the United States grew into a global awakening— a recognition that corruption, media manipulation, and elite control were not American problems alone, but universal ones.

People across continents saw in Trump not just a political figure, but a symbol—a man standing against a system designed to silence anyone who threatened its power. For years, other nations had suffered under similar forms of political dominance, media censorship, and institutional corruption. They saw what was done to Trump and realized something profound:

If they can do this to him, they can do this to any of us.

This realization sparked a worldwide shift—a movement of citizens, leaders, and nations demanding truth, sovereignty, and freedom.

THE WORLD SAW THE TRUTH BEHIND THE HEADLINES

For decades, the world viewed American media as the gold standard. If the news said it, it must be true. But Trump shattered that illusion. He showed the world how narratives were crafted, how stories were manipulated, and how truth was often buried beneath political agendas.

Nations began questioning the narratives their own media pushed. They recognized familiar tactics—smear campaigns, strategic leaks, coordinated attacks, and the labeling of truth-tellers as threats or extremists.

Across Europe, Latin America, Africa, and Asia, people awakened to the reality that media corruption was not local—it was global.

Trump unintentionally became the teacher.

A NEW ERA OF SOVEREIGNTY

One of Trump's most powerful messages was simple but revolutionary:

A nation must control its own destiny.

This message resonated worldwide. Leaders who long felt overshadowed by global institutions began asserting their independence. Nations that had accepted lopsided deals with larger powers began renegotiating. Countries that had been pressured into global alliances started walking away from agreements that harmed their citizens.

Trump inspired leaders across the world to:

- Put their borders first
- Prioritize their economies
- Protect their cultural identity
- Defend their sovereignty
- Question global institutions
- Challenge foreign influence
- Stand up to multinational elites

It wasn't "nationalism" in the negative sense; it was self-respect. The world began to understand that patriotism is not a crime—it is a responsibility.

THE PEOPLE RISE UP

From the streets of Europe to the towns of South America, millions of ordinary people felt a new sense of courage. They watched how Trump refused to bow to media pressure, how he withstood political persecution, and how he exposed the hidden alliances between governments, corporations, and unelected bureaucrats.

People realized they were not alone. Their struggles were not isolated. Their voices were not powerless.

Trump's fight gave them something rare—permission to speak out.

Millions began calling out corruption within their own governments. They challenged election fraud, media dishonesty, and foreign interference. They demanded transparency from institutions that had long operated in the dark.

A global awakening had begun. God was with him.

THE FEAR OF GLOBAL ELITES

The elites were rattled, not because Trump was a threat to world order, but because he was a threat to their order. The global establishment relied on:

- Weak leaders
- Compliant nations
- Predictable politics
- Controlled narratives
- Uninformed citizens

Trump disrupted all of it.

He proved that one leader, armed with conviction and truth, could destabilize the entire structure. He showed that global control was not invincible—it was only sustained by silence and compliance.

The elites feared one thing above all:

that other leaders would follow in his footsteps.

And many did.

TRUMP'S INFLUENCE ACROSS NATIONS

Whether they admitted it or not, world leaders began adjusting their strategies because of Trump.

Some strengthened their borders. Others renegotiated unfair trade deals. Many challenged global institutions. Several nations reduced reliance on foreign influence. Countless leaders adopted stronger, more assertive political styles.

Even leaders who publicly criticized Trump quietly adopted his tactics—leveraging national strength, renegotiating alliances, and demanding respect on the world stage.

Trump changed global leadership forever.

THE SPIRITUAL SIGNIFICANCE

Beyond politics, Trump's struggle awakened something deeper—a spiritual awareness. People saw the battle between truth and deception, light and darkness, freedom and control. They realized their nations were not just experiencing political problems, but moral ones.

Trump's resilience reminded people around the world that evil thrives only when good men do nothing. He reminded them that silence is surrender and that truth must be spoken even when it is costly.

His courage became a spark, igniting movements rooted not just in politics but in faith.

A WORLD FOREVER CHANGED

Whether one admired him or opposed him, one fact became undeniable:

Donald J. Trump changed the world.

He broke the illusion of global unity that had been built on deception. He exposed the mechanisms of control. He empowered the voiceless. He awakened nations to the power of sovereignty. And he gave millions the courage to stand up against systems designed to suppress them.

This is the legacy of the global awakening:

- People are no longer asleep.
- Nations are no longer compliant.
- The world is no longer blind.

And once a people awaken, they cannot return to bondage.

CHAPTER TWELVE – REDEMPTION AND LEGACY

Every leader leaves behind a footprint, but only a few leave behind a legacy. A legacy is not defined by popularity, media praise, or political favor. It is measured by impact—the kind of impact that shapes a nation's destiny and echoes through generations. Donald J. Trump's journey is one of the most complex, controversial, and consequential stories in American history, and his legacy is far from finished.

He began as the outsider—underestimated, mocked, dismissed. He faced a unified force of political, institutional, and media opposition designed to crush him. Yet he rose, resisted, and exposed a system that had been operating unchecked for decades. His journey from businessman to president, from hunted to hunter, became a narrative of resilience, courage, and profound purpose.

Trump's legacy is not simply political—it is cultural, spiritual, and generational.

A MAN TESTED BY FIRE

Every chapter of Trump's story is marked by trial. He endured investigations manufactured from thin air, media storms crafted to destroy, betrayals from those who claimed loyalty, and pressures that would have broken most men.

But the trials didn't weaken him. They revealed him.

Fire does not destroy solid gold—it purifies it. Pressure does not break the strongest steel—it strengthens it. Opposition does not derail the determined—it defines them.

Trump became a symbol of perseverance, rising each time the world declared him finished. His endurance became a form of redemption—not redemption from wrongdoing, but redemption through resilience. He proved that even when everything collapses around you, you can stand, fight, and ultimately prevail.

REDEMPTION THROUGH PURPOSE

Redemption is not always about forgiveness—often, it is about fulfillment. Trump's redemption was found in the realization of his purpose: exposing corruption, defending the forgotten, and restoring national pride. His trials made him stronger, but they also made him clearer. He no longer fought for himself; he fought for something far greater.

His purpose gave him a new kind of strength, one that transcended politics. He became the voice of millions who had long felt ignored, misunderstood, or oppressed by a system that claimed to represent them but never truly listened. Through Trump, they found not just a leader, but a redeemer of their hopes—someone who would not back down when the cost of truth became unbearable.

His redemption was tied to theirs.

THE LEGACY OF COURAGE

True courage is not found in avoiding conflict but in confronting it. Trump demonstrated a rare form of courage—the willingness to stand alone, to be hated, to be misrepresented, and to still speak the truth. Leaders throughout history have been praised for bravery on the battlefield, but Trump's battlefield was different:

It was fought in the media arena. It was fought in the halls of politics. It was fought in the court of public opinion. It was fought against the most powerful institutions in the world.

And yet he never surrendered.

His legacy is one of unshakeable courage—the kind that inspires future generations to stand for what is right, even when the entire world is shouting against them.

THE LEGACY OF AWAKENING

Perhaps the most profound legacy Trump leaves behind is the awakening of the American people. Before Trump, many believed corruption was a conspiracy theory, media bias was paranoia, and political manipulation was exaggerated. But after watching the unprecedented attacks against him, millions opened their eyes.

They realized:

- The system was not broken—it was working exactly as designed.
- The media was not informing—it was controlling.
- The elites were not serving—they were self-preserving.
- The justice system was not blind—it was selective.

Trump's fight awakened not only conservatives but people across the spectrum. He exposed truths that were never meant to be seen and raised questions that were never meant to be asked. And once the people saw behind the curtain, they could never unsee it.

The awakening is permanent.

THE LEGACY OF RESTORATION

Trump restored something America had lost:

- Pride in the nation.
- Faith in God.

- Faith in its potential.
- Hope for its future.

He brought patriotism back to the center of national identity. He reminded people that America is not defined by its flaws, but by its capacity to overcome them. He showed that leaders can serve their people without bowing to foreign pressure, corporate interests, or political corruption.

He restored belief in sovereignty, dignity, and the foundational truth that leaders should put their own citizens first.

THE LEGACY OF IMPACT BEYOND OFFICE

Unlike most presidents, Trump's influence did not end when he left the White House. It grew. His rallies expanded, his message intensified, and his support deepened. He became a movement, a symbol, and a moral force that transcended political office.

His enemies believed removing him from power would silence him. Instead, it amplified him.

Trump demonstrated a truth rarely seen in politics:

You don't need a position to have influence. You need purpose.

THE FUTURE OF HIS LEGACY

Redemption is not the end of the story—it is the beginning of legacy. Trump stands today not at the conclusion of his journey, but at the edge of a new chapter, one shaped by truth, conviction, and a nation forever transformed by his battle.

His legacy will be written in:

- The leaders he inspired, me.
- The movements he ignited
- The corruption he exposed
- The courage he awakened in millions
- The spirit of patriotism he restored

History will judge him not by the noise of his critics, but by the clarity of his purpose.

THE MAN WHO REFUSED TO BOW

In the end, Trump's legacy is not that he was perfect—but that he was unbreakable. He stood when others would have fallen. He fought when others retreated. He spoke truth when silence would have been easier. He carried the weight of a nation that fought against him and still refused to kneel.

That is the essence of redemption. That is the birth of legacy. That is the story of a man who changed the course of American history.

EPILOGUE – THE RETURN OF THE DEALMAKER

History is filled with moments when a leader rises, falls, and rises again. Not because circumstances change, but because purpose refuses to die. Donald J. Trump's journey has never been linear—it has been a fight, a storm, a trial by fire. Yet every time the world predicted his end, he emerged stronger, sharper, and more determined.

The hunted became the hunter.

The outsider became the leader.

The leader became the movement.

And the movement became the awakening of a nation.

But Trump's story does not conclude with the legacy he leaves behind. It continues in the chapter that stands before him—the chapter that history has not yet written, but destiny has already prepared.

This is not the epilogue of a finished life.

This is the beginning of a return.

THE MOMENT BETWEEN CHAPTERS

Every great leader faces a defining moment—the silent gap between one era and the next. It is the moment when the world goes quiet, when the noise fades, and when purpose becomes clear. Trump stands in such a moment now, looking not backward at the battles lost and won, but forward at the mission still unfinished.

He is older now, but not weaker. Wiser now, but not softer. Calmer now, but not silenced.

He carries the scars of political war, but also the unmatched experience of having faced the full strength of the world's most powerful institutions—and surviving.

In that survival lies the foundation of his return.

THE CALL THAT NEVER FADES

Great leaders are not driven by ambition alone. They are driven by calling. Trump's calling did not end when he left office. If anything, it grew louder.

He sees a nation in confusion, institutions in crisis, borders in chaos, and faith under attack. He sees a people more divided than at any time in recent memory—a division fueled by lies, fear, and manipulation. He sees a justice system twisted into a political weapon. He sees the same forces that once hunted him now hunting the American people.

And he feels the call to stand again.

The call is not political—it is moral. Not opportunistic—but necessary. Not for power—but for restoration. It is the call of a dealmaker who knows the battle is not over.

THE DEAL THAT REMAINS TO BE MADE

Trump has made deals on skyscrapers, global trade, foreign policy, and national reform. But one deal remains undone—the deal between America's past and America's future.

It is the deal to restore integrity to government. The deal to return power to the people. The deal to rebuild faith in truth. The deal to reclaim America's destiny.

Trump knows that this final deal cannot be made in boardrooms or negotiations alone. It requires courage, conviction, and a willingness to stand once more where the fire burns hottest. It requires a man who has walked through the flames and learned to embrace the heat.

THE WORLD WAITS

Across the United States—and across the world—millions are watching. Some watch in hope. Others watch in fear. But all watch with the knowledge that Trump's chapter is not yet closed.

Those who support him feel the anticipation. Those who oppose him feel the threat. Those who understand history feel the weight of the moment. They sense that Trump is not finished. They sense that destiny is calling him again. They sense that the return of the dealmaker is not a question of if—but when.

THE MAN WHO WON'T QUIT

If history has proven anything, it is this:

Trump is a man who refuses to quit.

He did not quit when the world laughed at him. He did not quit when the media smeared him. He did not quit when the system targeted him. He did not quit when his own allies betrayed him. He did not quit when he lost battles he should have won.

And he will not quit now.

Because this fight was never about him alone. It was—and still is—about America.

THE REAL HUNTER RETURNS

The hunter is not a man of revenge. He is a man of justice. A man of vision. A man of resolve. He hunts not people—but truth. Not enemies—but corruption. Not glory—but restoration. He hunts for the sake of a nation that was nearly taken from its people. He hunts for the generations that will inherit the consequences. He hunts for the God-given purpose that still burns inside him.

Trump's return is not about reclaiming a position. It is about reclaiming a mission.

THE FINAL WORD

The hunted has become the hunter. The movement has become a force. The force has become a legacy. And the legacy is becoming a return.

History rarely gives a man a second chance to correct what was stolen. But destiny often does. And destiny has not finished with Donald J. Trump.

The dealmaker is preparing. The nation is waiting. The world is watching. And the next chapter is about to begin. This is not the end. This is the return of the dealmaker.

www.ingramcontent.com/pod-product-compliance
Lightning Source LLC
Chambersburg PA
CBHW052120030426
42335CB00025B/3067